GEO

CHECKERBOARD SCIENCE LIBRARY

EVERYDAY INVENTIONS

CAMERAS

EVERYDAY INVENTIONS

ZOOM LENS   17-55mm   1:2.8

Φ77mm   LENS MADE IN JAPAN

Kristin Petrie
ABDO Publishing Company

visit us at
www.abdopublishing.com

Published by ABDO Publishing Company, 8000 West 78th Street, Edina, Minnesota 55439.
Copyright © 2009 by Abdo Consulting Group, Inc. International copyrights reserved in all
countries. No part of this book may be reproduced in any form without written permission from the
publisher. The Checkerboard Library™ is a trademark and logo of ABDO Publishing Company.

Printed in the United States.

Cover Photo: iStockphoto
Interior Photos: Alamy p. 17; AP Images p. 13; Canon Inc. p. 19; Corbis pp. 9, 22; Getty Images
    pp. 10, 23, 24, 27; iStockphoto pp. 1, 4, 5, 14–15, 15, 16, 18, 21, 25, 28, 29, 31;
    Peter Arnold p. 26

Series Coordinator: Megan M. Gunderson
Editors: Megan M. Gunderson, BreAnn Rumsch
Art Direction & Cover Design: Neil Klinepier

Library of Congress Cataloging-in-Publication Data

Petrie, Kristin, 1970-
  Cameras / Kristin Petrie.
    p. cm. -- (Everyday inventions)
  Includes bibliographical references and index.
  ISBN 978-1-60453-085-8
  1. Cameras--Juvenile literature. I. Title.

  TR250.P48 2009
  771.3--dc22

                    2008001558

CONTENTS

Cameras

Chances are, you know what you looked like as a baby. You could also tell someone what Mars looks like. And, you've probably seen creatures that live deep in the ocean.

How can you recognize all of these things? For this, you can thank the camera. With the help of cameras, you can see animals from Antarctica. You can look at cars from 1905 or capture a special moment from today.

Cameras are one of the most important inventions of all time. It took many great minds and numerous years to create this valuable tool. Keep reading to learn more about this wonderful invention.

Personal photographs remind us of where we've been and what we've done. They also show us who was there to share those experiences.

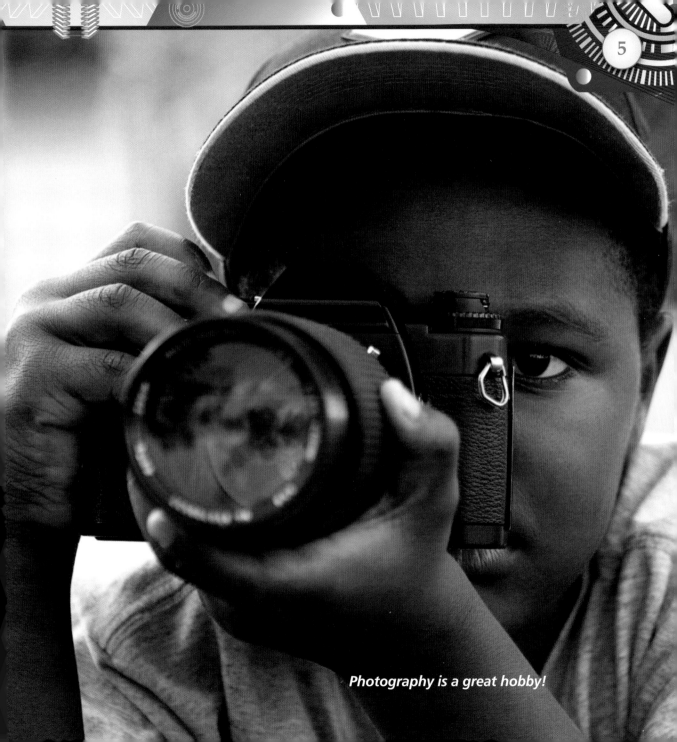

Photography is a great hobby!

Timeline

1727	Johann Heinrich Schulze discovered that silver salts darken when exposed to light.
1826	Joseph-Nicéphore Niepce used a light-sensitive metal plate in a camera obscura to create the first photograph.
1829	Niepce teamed up with Louis-Jacques-Mandé Daguerre, who soon invented the daguerreotype.
1884	George Eastman introduced roll film.
1924	Oskar Barnack created the lightweight, handheld Leica; Paul Vierkotter invented the first flashbulb.
1947	Edwin Herbert Land introduced the instant Polaroid Land Camera.
1962	The first exhibition of color photographs by one artist, Ernst Haas, was held at the Museum of Modern Art in New York City, New York.
1975	Eastman Kodak Company employee Steven Sasson invented the first digital camera.

Camera Facts

○ In 1858, French photographer Nadar created the first aerial photograph. It was taken from a balloon floating over Paris, France.

○ In the 1860s, Mathew Brady organized more than 100 photographers to cover the American Civil War. These important early photographers recorded everyday scenes of battlefields and military life. Brady's photographers left behind an invaluable record of the time period.

○ In the late 1800s, Eadweard Muybridge proved he had a talent for capturing movement on film. He developed an extremely fast shutter. And, he used many cameras to take numerous pictures quickly. Muybridge is especially famous for his series of photographs of a horse in motion. It proved that trotting horses lift all four legs off the ground at once!

Camera Obscura

The first cameras were nothing like the cameras of today. Thousands of years ago, a camera was just a hole in a wall! This tiny hole allowed a beam of light into a dark room. An image from outside was carried inside on that light beam. It was cast upside down on the far wall. This device was called a camera obscura, which means "dark chamber" in Latin.

By the 1500s, artists mainly used a camera obscura to trace images projected onto paper. In time, the camera obscura was reduced from a dark room to a small, dark box. Yet, how to permanently capture these projected images remained a mystery.

Drawing an image with the help of light is the basis of photography. In fact, the Greek words *photos* and *graphos* mean "light" and "writing." Photography is the art of using light to write on light-sensitive surfaces.

A modern camera permanently records images. But inside an early camera obscura, the image simply appeared upside down. This required an artist to sketch the image himself.

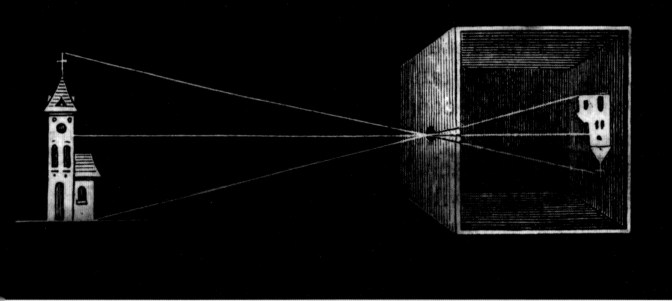

In 1727, German professor Johann Heinrich Schulze made an important discovery. He learned that **silver salts** darken when exposed to light. He used sunlight to record words on the salts. However, Schulze was not able to save his images. The goal of capturing and preserving real-life images was still out of reach.

Lasting Images

The first photograph was of a view from Le Gras, Niepce's house in Saint-Loup-de-Varennes, France.

French inventor Joseph-Nicéphore Niepce was ready for the challenge of making photographs permanent. In 1826, Niepce placed a light-sensitive metal plate in a camera obscura. After eight long hours, an image of his courtyard outside appeared. This was the first photograph!

In 1829, Niepce teamed up with fellow Frenchman Louis-Jacques-Mandé Daguerre. Niepce died four years later. But, Daguerre continued to improve their methods.

Soon, Daguerre discovered how to decrease a picture's exposure time to 30 minutes. He also learned how to make these images permanent using a salt mixture. *Daguerreotype* (duh-GEH-roh-tipe) became the name for his process and the photographs it made.

The daguerreotype process became very popular, but it had limitations. The pictures were small and heavy. They were also delicate and could not be copied. And, photographers needed a wagon full of equipment to take and process the photographs.

Around the same time, British inventor William Henry Fox Talbot invented light-sensitive paper. This allowed multiple prints of the same image to be made. However, Talbot's photographs were not as clear as daguerreotypes.

In 1884, American inventor George Eastman introduced a product to solve these problems. He had invented roll film, which was thin and light. Also, numerous pictures could be taken before a camera needed reloading.

In 1888, Eastman created an affordable, **portable** camera for his film. Finally, people could take pictures without a cartload of equipment!

Eastman's **portable** cameras were definitely more user-friendly. But, German inventor Oskar Barnack gets the credit for the first truly lightweight handheld camera. In 1924, he introduced the Leica. He combined his boss's name, Leitz, with the word *camera* to create its name.

Improvements in photography and camera technology continued. Thanks to Austrian engineer Paul Vierkotter, you can take pictures in the dark. He invented the first flashbulb in 1924. A camera's flash sheds light on your subject as the picture is taken.

Do you have an instant camera, such as a Polaroid? They work like magic! Point the camera, push a button, and out comes a fully developed picture! American inventor Edwin Herbert Land **demonstrated** this cool camera in 1947 for the Polaroid Corporation. He called it the Polaroid Land Camera. Today, we just call them Polaroids.

Camera technology and the art of photography continued to improve during the later 1900s. In 1962, Ernst Haas became the first artist to have a solo exhibition of color photographs. It was held at the Museum of Modern Art in New York City, New York.

Steven Sasson's first digital camera weighed eight pounds (4 kg)!

Then in 1975, Steven Sasson invented the first **digital** camera. He worked for the Eastman Kodak Company at the time. By the 2000s, digital cameras were a common feature of cellular telephones.

Bits and Pieces

The body of a camera is the box that holds the camera's **internal** parts. It does not let in any light unless you are taking a picture. A camera can be big or small, heavy or light. This all depends on the camera's options.

Every modern camera has a lens. The lens is made of curved pieces of glass or plastic. Its shape bends the light that bounces off your subject and enters your camera. The lens makes this **refracted** light form a clear image on your film.

You'll need to make sure your photographs aren't blurry! For some cameras, you turn the lens to focus. Other cameras focus for you. A lens also lets you zoom in like a telescope. Or, you can zoom out to capture a wider picture.

A camera lens concentrates incoming light. So, images take a short time to form. Some special cameras let in light but keep out water!

The camera's viewfinder is what you look through to find your subject. Some photographers look through an optical viewfinder. This is built into most cameras. In some cameras, a mirror reflects what your lens is seeing up to the viewfinder.

Digital cameras have a viewing screen. It looks like a small television screen. This feature lets you view your image before and after you take a picture.

Viewfinders and viewing screens let photographers see what the camera sees.

A camera's flash gives extra light to your picture. These electronic flashes allow you to take pictures in low light. So, you can take pictures inside and outside.

Stroboscopic flashes help slow down moving subjects for a camera. The process was first studied by Harold Edgerton in the 1930s. He took photographs of subjects such as flying hummingbirds. Their wings usually move too fast for the human eye to see. But, Edgerton was able to capture them on film.

Film comes in long rolls. To protect it from light, it is stored inside a **canister** called a film cassette.

Film advances one exposure at a time in the dark interior of a camera. Each time the shutter opens, a new part of the film is exposed to light.

Today, most people use color film, rather than black-and-white film. Color film has red, blue, and green **emulsion** layers. Each emulsion reacts only to its own color as it comes through the camera. Combined, these colors realistically re-create the subject of your photograph.

Parts of a Camera

APERTURE RING

SHUTTER RELEASE BUTTON

ZOOM LENS
28-105mm

FOCUSING RING

LENS

VIEWFINDER

FILM

MIRROR

BATTERIES

Focusing Light

The first step in taking a picture is up to you! You could just hold your camera in the air and shoot. But a better method is to locate your subject through the viewfinder. This is called framing. Now your camera knows what you want to photograph.

Next, your lighting must be adjusted. You may need artificial lights if it is dark. If you are close to your subject, the flash will do the job. Why is light so important? Light beams bounce off your subject to create its image in your camera.

When you press the shutter release button, light beams enter your camera through the lens. Shutter speed determines how long light passes into your camera. The shutter usually opens and closes quickly. The lens focuses the incoming light onto the film. That way, your image can be made quickly and clearly.

Inside, the light beams pass through the **aperture**. The aperture is a tiny hole that directs light to the film. Aperture

A large f-stop means a small aperture. It lets in less light than a small f-stop.

size is described using numbers called f-stops. Depending on its size, the **aperture** can let more or less light into the camera. When the light hits the film, your subject is recorded.

Developing Cameras

An early daguerreotype camera

Daguerreotype was the first popular type of photography. Inside a lightproof box was a heavy, silver-plated piece of copper. Light entered the camera through a lens and hit the copper plate. There, the light beams slowly created an image. This image could then be made permanent through a chemical process.

But a lighter, smaller material was desired. Roll film met this need. In 1888, this light-sensitive material had a paper backing. The following year, film had a plastic base. Either way, film was light and **portable**, just like the cameras that used it.

George Eastman holding a Kodak camera. The box camera's 100 pictures were round and measured approximately 2.5 inches (6.4 cm) across.

Roll film was used in the Kodak box camera. This simple camera had enough film for 100 pictures. It sold for about $25 in the late 1800s.

For another $10, the camera could be returned to the factory for developing. The factory made prints. Then, it sent back the camera with a new roll of film already loaded. One Kodak slogan read, "You press the button, we do the rest."

The Kodak Brownie was next. At just $1, this camera was even more affordable. And, it had removable film. This meant owners could send in just their film for developing.

The Polaroid Land Camera was next to steal the show. Light and chemicals mixed right inside the camera. This instant camera produced an image in less than a minute!

Camera recorders, or camcorders, became popular in the 1980s. These **portable** cameras record moving pictures and sound. Now, home movies of your family's favorite activities can be preserved.

Today, **digital** cameras are very popular. These cameras take pictures using a **charge-coupled device**, or CCD, rather than film.

Digital images are broken down into **pixels**. Each photograph becomes a number code that a computer can read. A computer translates the number code into an image. The image can then be produced on a screen for you to see and print.

With a modern instant camera, the photograph rolls out of the camera. This action causes chemicals on the film to combine and react. The reaction develops your picture instantly!

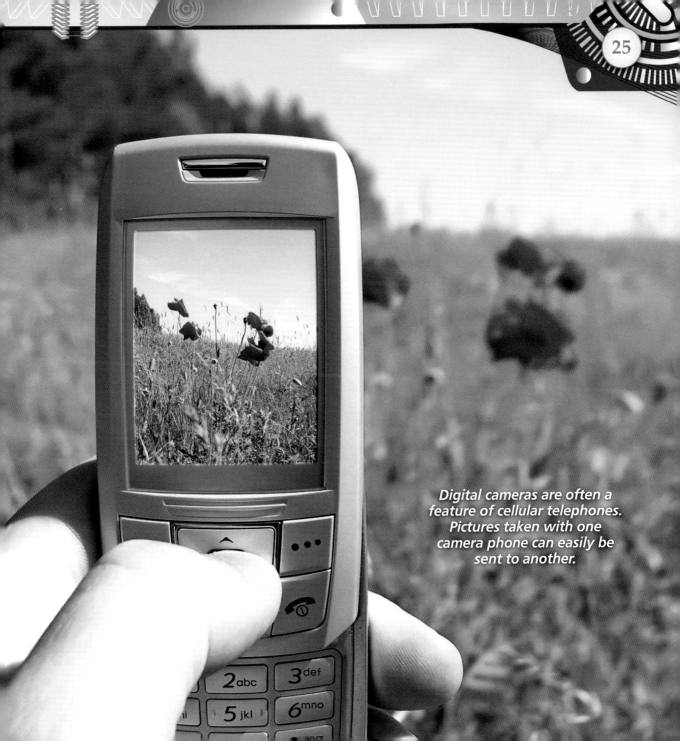

Digital cameras are often a feature of cellular telephones. Pictures taken with one camera phone can easily be sent to another.

Cameras at Work

Wildlife photography often benefits scientific research. This profession can take photographers to every continent, or even under the sea!

When most people think of who works with cameras, photographers come to mind. There are many types of professional photographers. Some focus their skills on people. They take family and individual portraits. Others capture animals and wildlife on film. Or, they may photograph new fashions and products for advertisements.

Photojournalists cover wars, sporting events, news conferences, and more. They may travel all over the world to report on important stories.

Photojournalists are also professional photographers. They capture entire events in pictures. Their work may cover a story that takes place over many days or even years.

Photographers in film production also tell a story. You see the work of these **cinematographers** in your favorite movies and television programs.

Other camera specialists may teach students about photography. Or, they may own a store that processes film and prints pictures. Some experts work in museums. They study the history of cameras and photography.

Finally, let's not forget the people who keep our cameras working. With today's high-tech cameras, repair specialists have a challenging job!

A Photo Finish

Cameras make life interesting! Thanks to cameras, you can see stars in space up close. You may even be able to see what your great-great-grandmother looked like. And, you can preserve memorable moments from your own life.

Some people believe cameras affect their privacy. True, a camera may detect a car racing through a red light. On the other hand, a fast camera can determine who won a race in a photo finish!

Many cities use red light cameras to encourage safe driving. Running a red light triggers a camera. The camera then photographs the car breaking the law.

Cameras have changed the way we live. **Satellite** cameras tell us what kind of weather to expect. X-ray photographs tell your dentist if you have cavities. Cameras can also be used to create stunning works of art. The past is remembered and the future is bright, thanks to the camera.

Sporting events such as horse races often rely on cameras to determine winners. Photo-finish cameras have been used at the Olympic Games since 1932.

GLOSSARY

aperture (AP-uhr-chur) - an opening, especially in a camera lens.

canister - a container used to hold a specific object, such as film.

charge-coupled device - an image sensor that builds up electric charges as light from an image hits it. The charges are then released as an electric current. This can be translated by computers and other devices to re-create the image.

cinematographer (sih-nuh-muh-TAH-gruh-fuhr) - a person who specializes in the art and science of photographing motion pictures.

demonstrate - to show or explain, especially by using examples.

digital - of or relating to numerical data that can be read by a computer.

emulsion (ih-MUHL-shuhn) - a light-sensitive coating on photographic film, plates, or paper.

internal - of, relating to, or being on the inside.

pixel - any of the small elements of brightness and color that, when combined, create a picture.

portable - able to be carried or moved.

refract - to change the path of something, such as light, especially as it passes from one medium to another.

satellite - a manufactured object that orbits Earth.

silver salts - a chemical mixture of salt and silver nitrate that darkens when exposed to light.

stroboscopic - relating to the use of a flashtube to light a moving object off and on.

WEB SITES

To learn more about cameras, visit ABDO Publishing Company on the World Wide Web at **www.abdopublishing.com**. Web sites about cameras are featured on our Book Links page. These links are routinely monitored and updated to provide the most current information available.

INDEX